100 facts
DINOSAURS

100 facts
DINOSAURS

Steve Parker

Miles
Kelly

First published in 2001 by Miles Kelly Publishing Ltd
Harding's Barn, Bardfield End Green, Thaxted, Essex, CM6 3PX, UK

This edition updated 2013, printed 2014

10 12 14 15 13 11 9 7

Publishing Director Belinda Gallagher
Creative Director Jo Cowan
Editorial Director Rosie Neave
Designer Venita Kidwai
Image Manager Liberty Newton
Production Manager Elizabeth Collins
Reprographics Stephan Davis, Jennifer Cozens, Thom Allaway
Assets Lorraine King

ISBN 978-1-84810-912-4

Printed in China

British Library Cataloguing-in-Publication Data
A catalogue record for this book is available from the British Library

ACKNOWLEDGEMENTS

The publishers would like to thank the following sources for the use of their photographs:
Key: t = top, b = bottom, c = centre, l = left, r = right, m = main

Cover: Roger Harris/Science Photo Library
Alamy: 29 (t) petpics **Corbis**: 12(t) Louie Psihoyos; 16 Layne Kennedy; 18(cl) Louie Psihoyos;
19 Sciepro/Science Photo Library; 29(b) Walter Myers; 33(t) Handout/Reuters; 42(b) Louie Psihoyos; 43(cr) Louie Psihoyos
Glow Images: 35(b) O. Louis Mazzatenta; 44(tl) Lynn Johnson/National Geographic Image Collection;
44(tr) Lynn Johnson/National Geographic Image Collection 45(l) Lynn Johnson/National Geographic Image Collection
Science Photo Library: 6–7 Jose Antonio Penas; 18–19 Julius T Csotony; 21 Jose Antonio Penas;
26–27 Christian Jegou Publiphoto Diffusion; 33(b) Christian Darkin; 36–37 Steve Munsinger;
38–39 Christian Jegou; 46(t) Natural History Museum, London **Shutterstock.com**: 8–9 Eric Broder Van Dyke; 9(t) Catmando;
10(b) leonello calvetti; 12–13 George Burba; 17(b) Catmando; 20 Michael Rosskothen; 21 Marilyn Volan;
22(t) Kostyantyn Ivanyshen; 22(c) Linda Bucklin; 23(bl) DM7; 23(br) Jean-Michel Girard; 30 leonello calvetti;
31(c) Ozja; 31(b) Ralf Juergen Kraft; 47 SmudgeChris **The Kobal Collection**: 41(b) Moonlighting Films

All other photographs are from:
Corel, digitalSTOCK, digitalvision, John Foxx, PhotoAlto, PhotoDisc, PhotoEssentials, PhotoPro, Stockbyte

Every effort has been made to acknowledge the source and copyright holder of each picture.
Miles Kelly Publishing apologizes for any unintentional errors or omissions.

Made with paper from a sustainable forest

www.mileskelly.net
info@mileskelly.net

The publishers would like to thank Dinosaur Isle for their help in
compiling this book.

Contents

World of the dinosaurs

1 For more than 160 million years, dinosaurs ruled the land. There were many different kinds – huge and tiny, tall and short, slim and bulky, fast and slow, with fierce sharp-toothed meat-eaters and peacefully munching plant-eaters. Then a great disaster ended their rule.

▼ In South America 70 million years ago, a group of *Austroraptor* dinosaurs attack a huge plant-eater. Many fast, fierce 'raptor' dinosaurs had feathers. *Austroraptor* was one of the largest raptors at 300-plus kilograms and 5 metres long.

When were dinosaurs alive?

2 The Age of Dinosaurs lasted from about 230 million to 65 million years ago, during a time called the Mesozoic Era. Dinosaurs were the main creatures on land for 80 times longer than people have been on Earth!

▼ Towards the end of the Palaeozoic Era, reptiles replaced amphibians as the main large land animals. Dinosaurs were in turn replaced in the Cenozoic Era by mammals. MYA means million years ago.

3 Dinosaurs were not the only animals living in the Mesozoic Era. There were many other kinds such as insects, spiders, shellfish, fish, scurrying lizards, crocodiles and furry mammals.

4 There were different shapes and sizes of dinosaurs. Some were small enough to hold in your hand. Others were bigger than a house!

◄ Tiny *Saltopus*, less than one metre long, was a Triassic close cousin of dinosaurs.

PALAEOZOIC ERA

The reptiles, including the ancestors of the dinosaurs, start to become more dominant than the amphibians.

Lystrosaurus (amphibian)

Diplocaulus (mammal-like reptile)

**299–251 MYA
PERMIAN PERIOD**

MESOZOIC ERA

The first true dinosaurs appear. These are small two-legged carnivores (meat-eaters), and larger herbivores, or plant-eaters.

Procompsognathus

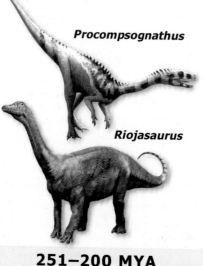

Riojasaurus

**251–200 MYA
TRIASSIC PERIOD**

Many different dinosaurs lived at this time, including the giant plant-eaters such as *Barosaurus*.

Barosaurus

Allosaurus

**200–145.5 MYA
JURASSIC PERIOD**

◀ *Stegosaurus* thrived during the late Jurassic Period, in North America and Europe.

6 There were no people during the Age of Dinosaurs. There was a gap of more than 60 million years between the last dinosaurs and the first humans.

5 No single kind of dinosaur survived for all of the Mesozoic Era. Many different types came and went. Some lasted for less than a million years. Other kinds, like *Stegosaurus*, kept going for many millions of years.

I DON'T BELIEVE IT!

The name 'dinosaur' means 'terrible lizard'. But dinosaurs weren't lizards, and not all dinosaurs were terrible. Small plant-eating dinosaurs were about as 'terrible' as today's sheep!

MESOZOIC ERA

During the last part of the Age of Dinosaurs, both giant carnivores and armoured herbivores were alive.

Tyrannosaurus rex

Deinonychus

Saltasaurus

Spinosaurus

145.5–65.5 MYA
CRETACEOUS PERIOD

CENOZOIC ERA

The dinosaurs have died out, and large mammals soon take over the land.

Megacerops herbivorous mammal

Newer kinds of mammals become more common, such as cats, horses, whales and bats.

Thylacosmilus carnivorous mammal

Nesodon herbivorous mammal

65.5–23 MYA
PALEOGENE PERIOD

23–2.6 MYA
NEOGENE PERIOD

Before the dinosaurs

7 **Dinosaurs were not the first animals on Earth.** Many other kinds of creatures lived before them, including different types of reptiles – the group that includes dinosaurs.

▶ *Erythrosuchus* was a crocodile-like reptile that lived before dinosaurs were common.

8 ***Dimetrodon* was a fierce, meat-eating reptile.** Although it looked like a dinosaur it wasn't one. It lived 270 million years ago, well before the dinosaurs arrived. *Dimetrodon* was about 3 metres long and had a tall flap of skin like a sail on its back.

▶ *Dimetrodon*'s legs sprawled sideways from its body, like a lizard, rather than being underneath, as in dinosaurs.

9 **Early crocodiles also looked like dinosaurs.** Crocodiles were around even before the first dinosaurs. One was *Erythrosuchus*, which was 4.5 metres long, lived 240 million years ago, lurked in swamps and ate fish.

10 Therapsids were around before the dinosaurs, and they also lived alongside the early dinosaurs. They were mammal-like reptiles because they didn't have scaly skin like most reptiles. Instead they had furry or hairy skin like mammals.

11 The dinosaur group probably appeared 238–232 million years ago. Lack of fossils means no one is sure when, where, or what were the ancestors. However it is known that the dinosaurs' closest relations include crocodiles and the flying reptiles called pterosaurs, all making up the bigger group termed archosaurs.

▶ *Euparkeria* could probably rear up to run on just its two rear legs — like many meat-eating dinosaurs later.

12 Some small reptiles show what the dinosaurs' ancestors could have looked like. They include *Euparkeria* in South Africa 245 million years ago, and *Lagosuchus* and *Marasuchus* in South America around 235 million years ago. They were small, light and fast, with long back legs, and sharp teeth for feeding on bugs and small creatures.

QUIZ

1. Did *Dimetrodon* live before or after the dinosaurs?
2. Did therapsids have scaly or furry skin?
3. What were the flying reptiles related to dinosaurs known as?
4. Did dinosaurs gradually change, or evolve into crocodiles?

Answers:
1. Before 2. Furry skin
3. Pterosaurs 4. Dinosaurs did not evolve into crocodiles, dinosaurs appeared afterwards

11

Dinosaurs arrive

13 The earliest dinosaurs stalked the Earth almost 230 million years ago. They lived in what is now Argentina, in South America. They included *Eoraptor* and *Herrerasaurus*. Both were slim and fast creatures. They could stand almost upright and run on their two rear legs. Few other animals of the time could run upright like this, on legs that were straight below their bodies. Most other animals had legs that stuck out sideways.

ACTUAL SIZE

▲ The teeth of *Eoraptor* were suited to eating both small animal prey and soft plant foods.

The long tail balanced the head and body over the rear legs

Large head with powerful jaws contained saw-edged teeth

Each foot had three long central toes with sharp claws, and a smaller, shorter toe to each side of these

▲ *Herrerasaurus* was about 3 metres long from nose to tail. It was small, light and fast.

14 Early dinosaurs hunted small animals such as lizards and other reptiles, insects and worms. They had lightweight bodies and long, strong legs to chase after prey. Their claws were long and sharp for grabbing victims. Their large mouths were filled with pointed teeth to bite and tear up their food.

▶ One of the early big dinosaurs, 2-tonne *Lessemasaurus* lived about 210 million years ago in South America.

15 As early dinosaurs spread over the land they began to change, or evolve, into new kinds. Evolution has happened in all living things since life began. New kinds of plants and animals appeared, thrived for a time, and then died out. Some of the early dinosaurs evolved to be much bigger and eat plants, like 9-metre-long *Lessemasaurus*.

STRONG LEGS!

You will need:
stiff card   sticky tape
safe scissors   split pins

1. Copy the picture of *Herrerasaurus* on page 12 onto card, without the rear legs. Colour it in on both sides and cut it out.

2. On another piece of card, copy the rear legs, colour them in and cut them out.

3. Fix the legs to the body, either side of the hip area, with the split pins. Adjust the angle of the body over the legs.

This is how many dinosaurs stood and walked.

First of the giants

16 One of the first big dinosaurs well-known from fossils was *Plateosaurus*. This plant-eater grew up to 8 metres long and lived almost 220 million years ago in what is now Europe. It could rear up on its back legs and use its long neck to reach food high in trees.

Long, flexible neck for reaching food high off the ground

Sharp, jabbing claws for defence

Long, strong tail for balance

▲ Fossils of more than 100 *Plateosaurus* have been found, so its size, shape, teeth and body details are well known compared to many other dinosaurs.

Powerful back legs for rearing up

17 *Riojasaurus* was an even larger plant-eater. It lived 218 million years ago in what is now Argentina. *Riojasaurus* was 10 metres long and weighed over one tonne – as much as a large family car of today.

Small head and long, flexible neck

18 The first big plant-eating dinosaurs may have become larger, with longer necks, so that they could reach up into trees for food.
Their great size would also have helped them fight enemies, since many other big meat-eating reptiles, some as long as 5 metres, were ready to make a meal of them.

◄ Like *Plateosaurus*, *Riojasaurus* was in the dinosaur group called prosauropods, with a small head, long neck and long tail.

19 These early dinosaurs lived during the first part of the Age of Dinosaurs – the Triassic Period.
By its end, 200 million years ago, dozens of kinds of dinosaurs roamed across much of the world.

I DON'T BELIEVE IT!

Early plant-eating dinosaurs did not eat fruits or grasses – there weren't any! They hadn't appeared yet. Instead they ate plants called horsetails, ferns, cycads and conifer trees.

What teeth tell us

20 We know about dinosaurs and other living things from long ago because of fossils. These are usually hard body parts, such as bones, claws, horns and scales, that are preserved in rocks for millions of years. Dinosaur teeth were very hard and formed many fossils.

22 The shape of a dinosaur's teeth help to show what it ate. *Edmontosaurus* was a 12-metre-long duck-billed dinosaur, and had rows of broad, wide, sharp-ridged teeth in the sides of its mouth. These were ideal for chewing tough plant foods like twigs and old leaves.

◄ The head of *Edmontosaurus* was long, broad and muscular, suited to spending hours chewing – similar to today's horse.

Toothless beak-like front of mouth

More than 500 chewing back teeth

21 *Tyrannosaurus* had 50–60 long, pointed teeth more than 20 centimetres long. These were excellent for tearing up victims, and for ripping off lumps of flesh for swallowing. As in other dinosaurs, all through life as old teeth broke or fell out, new ones grew in their place.

► *Tyrannosaurus* teeth were strong and stout, but not especially sharp-edged, more suited to tearing than slicing.

23 Some dinosaurs, such as *Gallimimus*, had no teeth at all! The mouth was shaped like a bird's beak and made of a tough, strong, horny substance like our fingernails. The beak was suited to pecking up all kinds of foods like seeds, worms and bugs, as many birds do today.

▲ *Gallimimus* was a type of 'ostrich dinosaur' with large eyes, a long, lightweight beak and long neck.

24 *Baryonyx* had narrow, pointed, cone-shaped teeth. These resemble the teeth of a crocodile or dolphin today. They were ideal for grabbing slippery prey such as fish.

▲ The head of *Baryonyx* was more than one metre long, with an expanded, spoon-shaped front snout.

25 The teeth of the giant, long-necked dinosaur *Apatosaurus* were shaped like pencils. They worked like a rake to pull leaves off branches into the mouth, for the dinosaur to swallow.

DINOSAUR TEETH!

With the help of an adult, look in a utensils drawer or tool box for dinosaur teeth! Some tools resemble the teeth of some dinosaurs, and do similar jobs.
File or rasp – broad surface with hard ridges, like the plant-chewing teeth of *Edmontosaurus*.
Knife – long and pointed, like the meat-tearing teeth of *Tyrannosaurus rex*.
Pliers – Gripping and squeezing, like the beak-shaped mouth of *Gallimimus*.

▲ Although *Apatosaurus* was about 25 metres long, its skull measured just 60 centimetres. It spent most of its time feeding.

Super-size dinosaurs

26 The true giants of the Age of Dinosaurs were the sauropods. These vast dinosaurs all had a small head, long neck, barrel-shaped body, long tapering tail and four pillar-like legs. The biggest sauropods included *Brachiosaurus, Mamenchisaurus, Barosaurus, Diplodocus, Futalognkosaurus* and *Argentinosaurus*.

◄ Fossil footprints from a sauropod herd near Purgatoire River, Colorado, USA.

27 Sauropod dinosaurs probably lived in groups or herds. We know this from their footprints, which have been preserved as fossils. Each foot left a print as large as a chair seat. Hundreds of footprints together showed many sauropods walked along with each other.

▲ *Futalognkosaurus*, a type of sauropod known as a titanosaur, was more than 30 metres long. Its name, given in 2007, means 'giant chief lizard' in the local Argentinian language.

Diplodocus is also known as 'Old Whip-tail'! It may have swished its long tail so hard and fast that it made an enormous CRACK like a whip. This living, leathery, scaly whip would scare away enemies or even rip off their skin.

28

Sauropod dinosaurs swallowed pebbles – on purpose! Their peg-like teeth could only rake in plant food, not chew it. Pebbles and stones gulped into the stomach helped to grind and crush the food. These pebbles, smooth and polished by the grinding, have been found with the fossil bones of sauropods.

▶ *Brachiosaurus* was about 25 metres long and probably weighed in the region of 30 tonnes. Its amazingly long neck allowed it to browse from the tallest trees.

29

The biggest sauropods like *Brachiosaurus* and *Futalognkosaurus* were enormous beasts. They weighed up to ten times more than elephants of today. Yet their fossil footprints showed they could run quite fast – nearly as quickly as you!

30

Sauropods probably had to eat most of the time, 20 hours out of every 24. They had enormous bodies that would need great amounts of food, but only small mouths to gather the food.

Killer claws

31 Nearly all dinosaurs had claws on their fingers and toes. These claws were shaped for different jobs in different dinosaurs. They were made from a tough substance called keratin – the same as your fingernails and toenails.

32 *Hypsilophodon* had strong, sturdy claws. This small 2-metre-long plant-eater probably used them to scrabble and dig in soil for seeds and roots.

33 *Deinonychus* had long, hooked claws on its hands. These helped it to grab victims and tear at their skin and flesh. It also had a huge hooked claw, as big as your hand, on the second toe of each foot. This could flick down like a pointed knife to slash pieces out of prey.

◄ *Deinonychus*, meaning 'terrible claw', probably had feathers like other raptors. It lived in North America 110 million years ago.

Long claw on each of the three fingers

Second toe had slashing 'terrible claw'

34 *Baryonyx* also had a large claw, but this was on the thumb of each hand. It may have worked as a fish-hook to snatch fish from water.

35 *Iguanodon* had claws on its feet. But these were rounded and blunt and looked more like hooves. There were also stubby claws on the fingers, while the thumb claw was longer and shaped like a spike, perhaps for stabbing enemies.

▶ Therizinosaurs, from the Cretaceous Period in Eastern Asia and Western North America, had enormous finger claws – why is a mystery.

36 Giant sauropod dinosaurs had almost flat claws. Dinosaurs such as *Apatosaurus* looked like they had toenails on their huge feet!

▶ The long claw on *Apatosaurus'* front foot was possibly for self defence.

37 The biggest claws of any dinosaurs, and any animals, belonged to the scythe dinosaurs or therizinosaurs. Their hand claws, up to one metre long, were perhaps used to pull down and cut off leafy branches as food.

38 Therizinosaurs were big, strange-looking dinosaurs, reaching 10 metres long and 5 tonnes in weight. They lived late in the Age of Dinosaurs, and the group included *Alxasaurus, Nothronychus, Beipiaosaurus* and *Therizinosaurus*.

Deadly meat-eaters

Spinosaurus lived about 100 million years ago. It grew to 15 metres in length, and weighed as much as 10 tonnes.

About 13–14 metres in length, Carcharodontosaurus hunted across North Africa 95 million years ago. Its saw-edged teeth were 20 centimetres long.

Giganotosaurus was up to 13.5 metres long and had the largest skull of any meat-eating dinosaur. It lived about 97 million years ago.

39 The biggest meat-eating dinosaurs were the largest predators ever to walk on Earth. *Allosaurus*, which lived 150 million years ago in North America, reached almost 10 metres in length, while *Tyrannosaurus rex* from 66 million years ago was 12 metres. In South America, *Giganotosaurus* was slightly larger, while in North Africa, *Carcharodontosaurus* and *Spinosaurus* were even bigger – the largest meat-eating dinosaurs known so far.

Some meat-eating dinosaurs not only bit their prey, but also each other! Fossils of several *Tyrannosaurus* had bite marks on the head. Perhaps they fought each other to become chief in the group, like wolves do today.

40 These great predators were well equipped for hunting large prey — including other dinosaurs. They had massive mouths with long sharp teeth in powerful jaws. They also had long, strong back legs to run fast, and enormous toe claws for kicking and holding down victims.

41 Meat-eaters probably got food in various ways. They hid behind rocks or trees and rushed out to surprise a victim. Some chased their prey, and others would plod steadily over time to tire out their meal. They might even scavenge — feast on the bodies of creatures that were dead or dying from old age, illness or injury.

T rex was among the last of the great predatory dinosaurs. It probably weighed 6–7 tonnes when fully grown.

Allosaurus was the largest meat-eating dinosaur of the Jurassic Period. It was a relative lightweight at only 2–3 tonnes!

Look! Listen! Sniff!

42 **Like the reptiles of today, dinosaurs could see, hear and smell the world around them.** We know this from fossils. The preserved fossil skulls had spaces for eyes, ears and nostrils.

43 **Some dinosaurs, such as *Leaellynasaura* and *Troodon*, had big eyes.** There are large, bowl-shaped hollows in their fossil skulls to allow for them. Today, animals such as mice, owls and night-time lizards can see well in the dark. Perhaps *Troodon* prowled through the forest at night, peering in the gloom for small creatures to eat.

▶ *Troodon* was about 2 metres long and lived in North America 70 million years ago.

▶ *Leaellynasaura*, was a 3-metre-long plant-eater from 115 million years ago in what is now Australia.

44 **There are also spaces on the sides of the head where *Troodon* had its ears.** Dinosaur ears were round and flat, like the ears of other reptiles. *Troodon* could hear the tiny noises of little animals moving about in the dark.

45 The nostrils of *Troodon*, where it breathed in air and smelled scents, were two holes at the front of its snout. With its delicate sense of smell, *Troodon* could sniff out its prey of insects, worms, little reptiles such as lizards, and small shrew-like mammals.

46 Dinosaurs used their eyes, ears and noses not only to find food, but also to detect enemies – and each other. *Parasaurolophus* had a long, hollow, tube-like crest on its head. Perhaps it blew air along this to make a noise like a trumpet, as an elephant does today with its trunk.

47 Dinosaurs such as *Parasaurolophus* may have made noises to send messages to other members of their group or herd. Different messages could tell the others about finding food or warn them about enemies.

▼ *Parasaurolophus* was a 'duck-billed' dinosaur or hadrosaur. It was about 10 metres long and lived 80 million years ago in North America.

Living with dinosaurs

48 All dinosaurs walked and ran on land, as far as we know. No dinosaurs could fly in the air or spend their lives swimming in the water. But many other creatures, which lived at the same time as the dinosaurs, could fly or swim. Some were reptiles, like the dinosaurs.

49 Ichthyosaurs were reptiles that lived in the sea. They were shaped like dolphins, long and slim with fins and a tail. They chased after fish to eat.

50 Plesiosaurs were sea–dwelling reptiles. They had long necks, rounded bodies, four large flippers and a short tail.

51 Turtles were another kind of reptile that swam in the oceans long ago. Each had a strong, domed shell and four flippers. Turtles still survive today. However ichthyosaurs and then plesiosaurs died out by the end of the Age of Dinosaurs.

▶ In this marine and shoreline Cretaceous scene, the dinosaurs *Ouranosaurus* (4) are shown living alongside lots of other types of animals.

52 Pterosaurs were reptiles that could fly. They had thin, skin-like wings held out by long finger bones. Some soared over the sea and grabbed small fish in their sharp-toothed, beak-shaped mouths. Others swooped on small land animals.

53 Birds first appeared about 150 million years ago. Some evolved to dive for fish in the sea, like gulls and terns today. *Ichthyornis* was about 25 centimetres long and lived along North American coasts.

▲ Unlike modern birds, *Ichthyornis* had tiny teeth in its jaws to grip slippery prey.

Key

1 *Hesperornis* (flightless bird)
2 *Elasmosaurus* (marine reptile)
3 *Pteranodon* (flying reptile)
4 *Ouranosaurus* (dinosaur)
5 *Archelon* (turtle, laying eggs)
6 *Archelon* (turtle, swimming)
7 *Kronosaurus* (marine reptile)
8 *Ichthyosaurus* (marine reptile)
9 Belemnoid (mollusc, similar to modern squid
10 *Mosasaurus* (marine reptile)
11 *Elasmosaurus* (marine reptile)
12 Ammonoid (mollusc)
13 *Cretoxyrhina* (shark)

54 Mosasaurs were huge, fearsome reptiles that appeared later in the Age of Dinosaurs. Related to lizards, they had a massive mouth full of sharp teeth. Some grew to 13 metres long and weighed over 5 tonnes.

How fast?

55 Dinosaurs walked and ran at different speeds, according to their size and shape. In the world today, cheetahs and ostriches are slim with long legs and run very fast. Elephants and hippos are huge heavyweights and plod along more slowly. Dinosaurs were similar. Some were big, heavy and slow. Others were slim, light and speedy.

QUIZ

Put these dinosaurs and modern animals in order of top running speed, from slow to fast.

Human (40 kilometres an hour)
Cheetah (100-plus kilometres an hour)
Muttaburrasaurus (15 kilometres an hour)
Ornithomimus (70 kilometres an hour)
Sloth (0.2 kilometres an hour)
Coelophysis (30 kilometres an hour)

Answer:
Sloth, *Muttaburrasaurus*, *Coelophysis*, Human, *Ornithomimus*, Cheetah

▼ *Ornithomimus*, from North America 70–65 million years ago, had long, powerful back legs, and hollow bones (like a bird) to save weight.

56 The fastest dinosaurs were the ostrich dinosaurs, or ornithomimosaurs. They had a similar body shape and proportions to today's biggest and fastest-running bird, the ostrich. *Ornithomimus* was one of the largest, up to 5 metres long and 300 kilograms in weight.

57 *Muttaburrasaurus* was a huge ornithopod type of dinosaur, a cousin of *Iguanodon*. It probably walked about as fast as you, around 4 to 5 kilometres an hour. It might have been able to gallop along at a top speed of 15 kilometres an hour, making the ground shake with its 3-tonne weight!

Ankle bones

Foot bones

► Fossils of *Muttaburrasaurus* come from Queensland, Australia. This bulky plant-eater had three large toes on each back foot and also three on the smaller front foot.

Toe bones ended in rounded claws

▼ *Coelophysis* was 3 metres long. It was one of the earliest dinosaurs, living about 220 million years ago.

58 *Coelophysis* was a slim, lightweight dinosaur. It could probably trot, jump and dart about with great agility. Sometimes it ran upright on its two back legs. Or it could bound along on all fours like a dog at more than 30 kilometres an hour.

Built like tanks

59 Some dinosaurs had body defences against predators. These might be large horns and spikes, or thick, hard lumps of bone like armour-plating. Most armoured dinosaurs were plant-eaters. They had to defend themselves against big meat-eating dinosaurs such as *Tyrannosaurus*.

60 *Triceratops* had three horns, one on its nose and two much longer ones above its eyes. It also had a wide shield-like piece of bone over its neck and shoulders. The horns and neck frill made *Triceratops* look very fearsome. But most of the time it quietly ate plants. If attacked, *Triceratops* could charge and jab with its horns, like a rhino today.

▼ *Triceratops* was 9 metres long and weighed more than 5 tonnes. It lived 65 million years ago in North America.

Wide neck frill of bone and skin

Long, sharp brow horns

Smaller nose horn

Sharp beak-shaped front of mouth

Wide feet spread great body weight

DESIGN A DINOSAUR!

Make an imaginary dinosaur. It might have the body armour and tail club of *Euoplocephalus*, or the head horns and neck frill of *Triceratops*. You can draw your dinosaur, or make it out of pieces of card or from modelling clay. Give it a made-up name, like *Euoploceratops* or *Tricephalus*. How well protected is your dinosaur? How does it compare to some armoured creatures of today, such as tortoises, armadillos or porcupines?

61 *Styracosaurus* was a ceratopsian ('horn face') dinosaur, like *Triceratops*, but with a more elaborate neck frill. Up to six horns as long as one metre extended from the frill's edge, giving this dinosaur an even fiercer appearance.

Tail club made from several fused (joined) bones

Long, straight, powerful tail to swing club

Back covered with bony plates set within the skin

▲ *Styracosaurus* grew up to 6 metres long and was 1.8 metres tall at the shoulder.

62 *Euoplocephalus* had a great lump of bone on its tail. This measured almost one metre across and looked like a massive hammer or club. *Euoplocephalus* could swing it at predators to protect itself from attack.

◀ *Euoplocephalus* belonged to the group called ankylosaurs. With big bony sheets and lumps in their skin, they were the most armoured of all dinosaurs.

Nests and eggs

63 Like most reptiles today, dinosaurs produced young by laying eggs. These hatched out into baby dinosaurs that gradually grew into adults.

64 Many kinds of dinosaur eggs and babies have been found. These include those of small, strong-beaked *Oviraptor* from Central Asia and the early sauropod *Massospondylus* from South Africa.

65 Different dinosaurs laid different sizes and shapes of eggs. Huge sauropod dinosaurs such as *Brachiosaurus* probably laid rounded eggs as big as basketballs. Eggs of big meat-eaters like *Tyrannosaurus* were more sausage-shaped, 40 centimetres long and 15 centimetres wide.

66 Some dinosaurs made nests for their eggs. *Oviraptor* lived more than 75 million years ago in what is now the Gobi Desert of Asia. It probably scraped a bowl-shaped nest in the soil about one metre across. Into this it laid about 15–20 eggs, in a neat spiral shape.

▼ This female *Oviraptor* is checking the newly laid eggs in her nest. Each egg is 14–18 centimetres long.

▲ Studying preserved unhatched eggs (real fossil, left) shows they contained tiny baby dinosaurs (artist's drawing, right).

67 Dinosaur eggs probably hatched after a few weeks or months, depending on how warm it was. The eggshells were slightly leathery and bendy, like most reptile eggshells today, and not brittle or hard like the shells of modern birds' eggs.

▶ Seventy–five million years ago in East Asia, pig–sized *Protoceratops* prepares to defend its nest and eggs from a hungry *Velociraptor*.

68 Fossils of baby dinosaurs show that they looked very much like their parents. However the neck frill of a baby *Protoceratops* was not as large when compared to the rest of its body, as in the adult. As the youngster's body grew, the frill grew faster, so its relative size changed. Other dinosaurs' body proportions also changed as they grew bigger.

69 Recent fossil finds show that some dinosaurs looked after their babies, like some reptiles today, such as crocodiles. In one discovery, an adult *Protoceratops* was preserved with some babies just 10–15 centimetres long, probably less than one year old.

Dinosaur babies

70 **Some dinosaur parents may have fed their young.** Fossils of duckbilled *Maiasaura* include nests, eggs and newly hatched young. The hatchlings could not move around because their leg bones were not strong enough. Yet their tiny teeth had slight scratches and other marks from eating food. So the parent *Maiasaura* probably brought food, such as leaves and berries, to the nest for them.

▼ In 1978 more than 200 fossils of *Maiasaura* nests, eggs, babies, youngsters and adults were found at a site now known as 'Egg Mountain' in Montana, USA. They date to around 75 million years ago.

▲ *Maiasaura* was a plant-eater about 9 metres long, belonging to the hadrosaur group. Its newly hatched babies were only 40 centimetres long, but within a year they had grown to 150 centimetres.

71 **The nest of *Maiasaura* was a mud mound about 2 metres across, with 30–40 eggs and babies.** Some fossils show unhatched eggs broken into many small parts, as though squashed by the babies that had already hatched out.

Baby dinosaurs grew up to five times faster than human babies. A baby sauropod dinosaur like *Diplodocus* was already one metre long and 8 kilograms in weight when it hatched from its egg!

72 Some dinosaurs may even have cared for their young after they left the nest. *Psittacosaurus* was a 2-metre-long plant-eater that lived 130–100 million years ago in East Asia. One set of fossils from China suggests that one adult was guarding 34 babies when they all died together, perhaps because the tunnel they were hiding in collapsed.

▼ Fossils of *Psittacosaurus* found in 2003 suggest that one adult may have looked after more than 30 babies.

The end for the dinosaurs

73 About 65 million years ago, the Age of Dinosaurs came to a sudden end. Fossils preserved in the rocks show great changes at this time. However the fossils also show that creatures like fish, insects, birds and mammals carried on. What happened to kill off some of the biggest, most successful animals the world has ever seen? There are many ideas. It could have been one disaster, or a combination of several.

74 The disaster may have been caused by a giant lump of rock, an asteroid or meteorite. This came from outer space and smashed into the Earth. The impact threw up vast clouds of water, rocks, ash and dust that blotted out the Sun for many years. Plants could not grow in the gloom, so many plant-eating dinosaurs died. This meant meat-eaters had less food, so they died as well.

75 Many volcanoes around the Earth could have erupted all at the same time, perhaps due to the meteorite impact. They threw out red-hot rocks, ash, dust and poison gas. Creatures would have choked and died in the gloom.

▼ Scientific studies show that 65.5 million years ago, a space rock smashed into Earth near what is now Yucatan, Mexico.

76 The disaster might have involved a terrible disease. Perhaps this gradually spread among certain kinds of animals and killed them off.

METEORITE SMASH!

You will need:
plastic bowl   flour   large pebble
desk lamp

Put the flour in the bowl. This is Earth's surface. Place the desk lamp so it shines over the top of the bowl. This is the Sun. The pebble is the meteorite from space. Drop the pebble into the bowl. See how the tiny bits of flour float in the air like a mist, making the 'Sun' dimmer. A real meteorite smash may have been the beginning of the end for the great dinosaurs.

77 It might be that dinosaur eggs were eaten by a plague of animals. Small, shrew-like mammals were around at the time. They may have eaten the eggs at night as the dinosaurs slept.

What happened next?

78 Other kinds of animals died out with dinosaurs. Flying reptiles called pterosaurs, and swimming reptiles called mosasaurs and plesiosaurs, disappeared. Lots of plants died out too. When a group of living things dies out, it is called an extinction. When many groups disappear at the same time, it's known as a mass extinction.

79 Several groups of reptiles also survived the mass extinction. They include crocodiles and alligators, turtles and tortoises, lizards and snakes. Why some kinds died out in the great disaster, yet other types survived, is one of the main puzzles that experts today are still trying to solve.

80 Even though many kinds of animals and plants died out 65 million years ago, other groups lived on. Crabs, shellfish, insects, worms, fish, frogs and mammals all survived the mass extinction – and these groups are still alive today.

1 Coryphodon (browsing mammal)
2 Gastornis (flightless bird)
3 Eobasileus (browsing mammal)
4 Branisella (early monkey)
5 Tremacebus (early monkey)
6 Paraceratherium (browsing mammal)
7 Arsinoitherium (browsing mammal)

Key

8 Hyracotherium (early horse)
9 Andrewsarchus (carnivorous mamma
10 Eobasileus (browsing mammal)
11 Plesiadapis (early primate)
12 Ptilodus (squirrel–like mammal)
13 Chriacus (raccoon–like mammal)

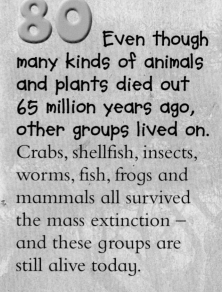

81 After the mass extinction, a different group of animals began to take over the land. These were the mammals. Through the Age of Dinosaurs they were mostly small and skulking, coming out only after dark. Now they could change or evolve to become bigger. Within a few million years they had developed into many kinds, from peaceful plant-eaters to huge, fierce predators.

▼ The mass extinction of 65 million years ago killed big dinosaurs and many other kinds of animals and plants. But plenty of animals survived, especially the mammals.

Myths and mistakes

82 **Some popular ideas about dinosaurs are probably not true.** For example, they are shown in bright colours such as red, yellow, green and blue. This is guesswork. For dinosaurs and other creatures, there are fossils of skin, and also fossilized feathers, as for *Confuciusornis*. But most, being fossils, have turned to stone, so they do not indicate colour. However a few well-preserved feathers show striped patterns, maybe in red and brown.

Toothless beak

Finger claws on wing

83 **For many years, people thought that all dinosaurs were slow and stupid animals.** But we cannot be sure. Some dinosaurs were quick and agile. Also some, like *Troodon*, had big brains for their body size. They may have been quite intelligent.

◄ Head-to-head butting, shown here by *Wannanosaurus*, is no longer thought likely.

84 **Another idea was that 'bone-headed' dinosaurs (pachycephalosaurs) crashed their heads together.** It was thought they did this when fighting for mates or to be leader of the herd, just like rams head-butt today. But their domed skulls would probably slip sideways as they thudded together, causing little damage. Maybe they butted each other in the sides instead.

20-centimetre-long wing feathers for agile flight

Wingspan of 70 centimetres

◀ Studies of fossil feathers from *Confuciusornis*, which lived 130 million years ago in China, suggest its plumage may have been red and black.

85 Another idea grew up that early cave people had to fight against dinosaurs and kill them – or the other way around. But they did not. There was a very long gap, more than 60 million years, between dinosaurs such as *Tyrannosaurus* and the earliest people.

86 Some people believe that dinosaurs may survive today in remote, faraway places on Earth, such as thick jungle or ocean islands. But most of the Earth has now been visited and explored, and no dinosaurs have been found alive.

Long streamer-like tail feathers may have been on the male only

▼ In the movie *The Dinosaur Project* (2012) explorers find living dinosaurs in Africa's Congo forest. However this is purely fiction.

I DON'T BELIEVE IT!

One dinosaur's thumb was put on its nose! When scientists first dug up fossils of *Iguanodon*, they found a horn-shaped bone, which fitted *Iguanodon*'s nose. Most scientists now believe that the spike was a thumb claw.

How do we know?

▼ Fossils form best in water, such as when drowned dinosaurs were washed by floods into a lake or sea.

1. After death, the dinosaur sinks to the river bed. Worms, crabs and other scavengers eat its soft body parts.

2. Sediments cover the hard body parts, such as bones and teeth, which gradually turn into solid rock.

87 **We know about long-gone dinosaurs mainly from the fossils of their body parts.** These took thousands or millions of years to form, usually on the bottoms of lakes, rivers or seas, where sand and mud can quickly cover the parts and begin to preserve them. If the animal died on dry land, its parts were more likely to be eaten or rot away.

88 **The body parts most likely to fossilize are the hardest ones, which rot away most slowly after death.** These include bones, teeth, horns and claws of dinosaurs and other animals, also plant parts such as bark, seeds and cones.

89 **Very rarely, a dinosaur or other living thing was buried soon after it died, then a few of the softer body parts also became fossils.** These include bits of skin or the remains of the last meal in its stomach.

▲ Bony lumps in the skin of armoured dinosaurs such as ankylosaurs fossilize well — the softer skin has rotted away.

3. Huge earth movements move, lift and tilt the rock layers so they become dry land.

4. Millions of years later the upper rock layers wear away and the fossil remains are exposed.

90

Not all dinosaur fossils are from the actual bodies of dinosaurs. Some are the signs, traces or remains that they left while alive. These include eggshells, nests, tunnels, footprints, and claw and teeth marks on food.

▲ Dino-dropping fossils come in many shapes and sizes! This scientist is an expert in their study.

QUIZ

Which body parts of a dinosaur were most likely to become fossils? Remember, fossils form from the hardest, toughest bits that last long enough to become buried in the rocks and turned to stone.

a. Skull bone b. Muscle c. Leg bone
d. Scaly skin e. Eye f. Blood
g. Claws h. Teeth

Answer:
a. Skull bone
c. Leg bone g. Claws h. Teeth

91

Dinosaur droppings also formed fossils! They are called coprolites and contain broken bits of food, showing what the dinosaur ate. Some dinosaur droppings are as big as a suitcase!

Digging up dinosaurs

▶ At the excavation site or dig, the first tasks are to make surveys by checking the rock for suitable signs of fossils.

◀ Small bits of rock are scraped away. Workers make notes, draw sketches and take photos to record every stage.

92 **Every year, thousands more dinosaur fossils are discovered.** Most of them are from dinosaurs already known to scientists. But five or ten might be from new kinds of dinosaurs. From the fossils, scientists try to work out what the dinosaur looked like and how it lived, all those millions of years ago.

93 **Most dinosaur fossils are found by hard work.** Fossil experts called palaeontologists study the rocks in a region and decide where fossils are most likely to occur. They spend weeks chipping and digging the rock. They look closely at every tiny piece to see if it is part of a fossil. However some dinosaur fossils are found by luck. People out walking in the countryside come across a fossil tooth or bone by chance.

94 Finding all the fossils of a single dinosaur neatly in position is very rare. Usually only a few fossil parts are found from each dinosaur. These are nearly always jumbled up and broken.

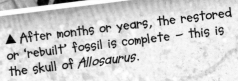
▲ After months or years, the restored or 'rebuilt' fossil is complete – this is the skull of *Allosaurus*.

◄ Brushes remove bits of dust, soil and rock flakes. Fragile fossils may be protected with 'jackets' of glass–fibre or plaster.

95 Dinosaur fossils are studied and rebuilt in palaeontology workrooms. They are cleaned and laid out to see which parts are which. It is like trying to put together a jigsaw with most of the pieces missing. Even those that remain are bent and torn. The fossils are put back together, then soft body parts that did not form fossils, such as skin, are added. Scientists use clues from similar animals alive today, such as crocodiles, to help 'rebuild' the dinosaur.

Dinosaurs today

96 The name 'dinosaur' was invented in 1842 by English scientist Richard Owen. He realized that the fossils of some prehistoric creatures were reptiles, but different from any known reptile group. So he made a new group, Dinosauria. Its first three members were *Iguanodon*, *Megalosaurus* and *Hylaeosaurus*, all from fossils found in England.

▲ Fossil *Sinosauropteryx* has long legs and feet, lower left. Its tail arches up and forwards to its skull, upper right.

▲ The dinosaur *Caudipteryx* from China had tiny arms and fanned-out tail feathers.

98 In 1996 fossils of the dinosaur *Sinosauropteryx* showed it had feathers. This slim, fast meat-eater, only one metre long, lived 123 million years ago in China. Its feathers were thin and thread-like, not designed for flying.

97 From the 1850s there was a rush to find hundreds of new dinosaurs in North America. In the 1920s exciting discoveries were made in Central Asia. Today, dinosaur remains are being found all over the world, even in frozen Antarctica. Some of the most amazing fossils in recent years come from Argentina and China.

▶ *Microraptor* was one of the smallest raptors ('thief' dinosaurs), just 80 cm long.

▲ Yutyrannus was one of the biggest feathered dinosaurs, and weighed almost 2 tonnes. Its fossils are 120 million years old and come from northeast China.

▼ Macaws and other birds are flying dinosaurs of today.

99 Following *Sinosauropteryx*, many more feathered dinosaurs have been found. These include turkey-sized *Caudipteryx*, tiny *Microraptor*, 2-metre *Dilong*, and the huge meat-eater *Yutyrannus*, at over 9 metres in length. But none of these creatures had bodies or feathers designed for flight. However *Archaeopteryx*, which lived 150 million years ago, was a small meat-eater with wide feathers just right for flight.

▶ An early cousin of *Tyrannosaurus*, *Dilong* was also much smaller, about 2 metres from nose to tail.

100 Most experts now believe that birds evolved from small meat-eating dinosaurs. The modern scientific view is that birds are part of the dinosaur group. This means not all dinosaurs died out, or went extinct, 65 million years ago. Some are alive today. They hop, flap and sing in our gardens, parks, wood, seashores and other habitats – they are birds.

I DON'T BELIEVE IT!
The dinosaur with shortest name was also one of the smallest. *Mei* (meaning 'sound asleep') had feathers and was less than 60 centimetres long.

Index